Gloria, The Gecko Attendant.

Written and Illustrated by Vanessa M. Castro

Everyday, thousands of children like Sabrina are born with disabilities, so they have friends like Gloria, the Gecko Attendant, to help them with their daily needs.

A person with a disability means that he or she has trouble either hearing, seeing, walking, or using their arms and legs. Sometimes their minds don't work in the usual way.

1

Sabrina has a disability called (CP) cerebral palsy. She has limited use of her arms and legs, so she uses a wheelchair. Sabrina is very smart and goes to school everyday, but she needs assistance on a daily basis in order to have an active normal life.

Sabrina's parents were looking for someone to help her. When they met Gloria through an agency, Gloria was a big green gecko wearing a red hat and matching red purse.

Sabrina and her parents had never seen anything like Gloria. Gloria sat down at the table with Sabrina, her parents, and the woman from the agency. The parents were shocked. "Hi Gloria. It's very nice to meet you."

"It's nice to meet you too."

"Have you ever worked with a person with a disability before?" Sabrina's dad asked Gloria.

"No, but I'm certainly willing to try."

Sabrina's mother started explaining,

"Since Sabrina has CP, she uses a power wheelchair to get around. She also has difficulty speaking clearly, and only a few people are able to understand her. She has a special computer that she uses as a communication device. Sabrina types, and the computer speaks. Sometimes it's hard to understand, so you will need to read the screen. Gloria, you will have to be patient and wait for her to finish. It takes time. Can you do that?"

Sabrina's mother continued, "Every morning after you get Sabrina in her wheelchair, she will type out what she wants to do that day."

"Okay. I understand." Said Gloria.

They looked at Sabrina waiting for her to decide if she would give Gloria, the gecko, a chance.
Sabrina couldn't stop smiling.

With excitement, Sabrina yelled out, "Yes! I want Gloria!"

Gloria gave Sabrina a big hug to thank her.

On Gloria's first day, Sabrina woke up, and saw Gloria standing in a giant red bowl of pasta that was overflowing. Sabrina was stunned. Pasta was everywhere, in the air, on the bed, on the floor, and in Sabrina's hair.

Gloria stepped out of the pasta bowl, yawned and stretched her arms, and said, "Good morning Sabrina. Are you ready to get up?"

Sabrina nodded yes and pointed to the pasta bowl.

"Oh, are you wondering about the pasta bowl?" Gloria asked.

Sabrina nodded yes.

Gloria explained, "I am an Italian gecko. I lived in Italy for many years. When I was a baby, I'd crawl around and find pasta on the ground. I ate a lot of pasta. When I got tired and full, I gathered up what was left and made a pasta bed to sleep on it. It was very comfortable."

Sabrina laid in bed laughing.

"Give me fifteen minutes to clean up and get my pasta bowl out of your room and then I'll get you up.   Is that cool with you?" Gloria asked.

Sabrina smiled and said, "Yes."

She laid in bed watching Gloria clean up and stuff three big black garbage bags with pasta.

When Gloria pushed her giant pasta bowl outside to the backyard, she said to herself,

Once she got outside, Gloria covered the bowl with foil so that the pasta would stay fresh and soft.

Sabrina's mom came out and told Gloria that she was welcome to sleep in the bed in the guestroom."

"I know. Thanks. I just prefer sleeping in pasta."

"Okay, as long as you are comfortable."

Gloria then headed back to Sabrina's bedroom. She yawned and stretched as she started getting Sabrina ready for the day.

Sabrina is unable to use the bathroom by herself, so Gloria carried her into the bathroom and helped her on the toilet.

While Sabrina sat on the toilet, Gloria brushed her teeth.

Splish - Splash.
Gloria then gave her a nice warm bath.

16

Gloria then wrapped a towel around Sabrina, carried her to the room, put her in a chair, and helped pick out her outfit for the day. Once Sabrina chose her clothes, Gloria got her dressed.

Gloria lifted Sabrina up and put her in the wheelchair.

These are simple tasks for most people. However, Sabrina would not be able to do any of these things by herself.

Dressed, and in her wheelchair with the talking computer, Sabrina was finally able to tell Gloria what she wanted to do that day.

When Sabrina talks on the phone, she uses her talking computer. It's often difficult for the person on the other end of the line to hear the computer, so Gloria translates what Sabrina says.

Next Gloria cooked lunch. Sabrina loves pasta, so Gloria made her spaghetti and meatballs.

"Not only do I sleep in pasta, I'm an expert at making fresh Italian pasta. You will love my spaghetti."

Sabrina also needs help feeding herself, so Gloria sat down at the table and fed her spaghetti and meatballs.

After lunch, Gloria washed the dishes and cleaned up the kitchen.

Then Sabrina wanted to check her email, so Gloria helped her log in.

While Sabrina is on her computer, Gloria did some house chores. She likes to multitask, so Gloria vacuumed and washed the windows at the same time.

Sabrina was amazed and typed out, "WOW! None of my other attendants could vacuum and wash the windows at the same time."

"That's because I'm a super awesome gecko attendant. Plus, when we multitask, we get more things done quicker."

As she turned on the washing machine and started doing laundry, Gloria thought to herself,

"Geez-Louise, this girl has a ton of clothes."

When Sabrina finished her homework and Gloria finished the house chores, Sabrina wanted to go shopping.

Gloria said, "That's a brilliant idea. You need groceries. Do you want to go to Safeway?"

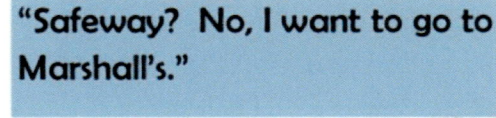

"Safeway? No, I want to go to Marshall's."

"Marshall's?" Gloria asked laughing. "Why? I just washed and folded all of you clothes. And Girl, you have a ton of clothes."

"Yeah, but I want a new dress for dinner tonight."

"Dinner? What dinner tonight?" Gloria was completely confused.

27

"Oh, didn't I tell you? We're meeting my friends for dinner at Giovanni's at 5:00."

"Who are we having dinner with?" Gloria was curious.

"Oh just Tiffany, Sheila, Tony, Ben, and I'm not sure who else."

Gloria said, "What about Safeway? You need food, Girlie."

"Okay, we can go to Safeway after Marshall's or tomorrow."

"You said we have to be at Giovanni's at 5:00, right?"

Sabrina said, "Yeah, 5:00."

28

Gloria looked at the clock and said, "Hieyayaya. Okay, we better get going." She grabbed her red hat and purse and asked Sabrina which jacket she wanted.

Sabrina said, "Yellow."

Gloria grabbed her yellow jacket, got Sabrina into her wheelchair accessible van, and off too Marshall's they went.

After an hour, Sabrina decided to get a pretty yellow dress like the one in the store window.

Gloria checked her watch and said, "We definitely don't have time to go to Safeway. We better get home and get you dressed if we have to be at Giovanni's by 5:00."

"Sounds good to me. Let's go!" Sabrina typed out smiling.

When they arrived at the restaurant, they opened the door and instantly smelled the delicious food. Their mouths began to water as their stomachs growled.

Six of Sabrina's friends came to dinner. They had pizza, pasta, strawberry punch, and ice cream for dessert.

Sabrina typed, "This was a great night! Thanks everyone for coming!"

Once they got home, Gloria changed Sabrina into her pajamas and said, "It was a great day and a fun night. I think I will really like this job."

Sabrina smiled.

As Gloria tucked Sabrina into bed, she said, "Good night, Girlie. Remember, we have to go to Safeway or you will starve."

Sabrina laughed as they hugged good night.

Made in the USA
Columbia, SC
22 November 2018